TABLE OF CONTENTS

I0409962

i

LIST OF TABLES

U.S. STRATEGY TOWARDS NORTH KOREA

The United States' containment policy imposed upon North Korea has been successful for 50 years. This post–World War II strategy has prevented a major war since the conclusion of the Korean Conflict. Our changing world environment characterized by globalization; end of the Cold War; increased numbers of failed and non-state actors; rise of terrorist and religious extremist groups; proliferation of weapons of mass destruction (WMD); and associated missile exportation and technology transfer mandates that the nation reexamine its current strategy to deal with these emerging threats to our national security. This paper conducts an analysis of current U.S. policy towards North Korea and recommends necessary changes.

One should view the Korean situation in the context of a larger "ends-ways-means" analysis. U.S. national interests (ends) in the Asian-Pacific region are diverse. They include the ability to deter and defeat aggression against any U.S. friend and ally; defeat terrorist organizations; maintain economic vitality of the region; provide free market access to the region; prevent proliferation of WMD; preclude state failure and internal conflict; and promote democracy and adherence to human rights agreements.[1] A strategy of containment (ways) has maintained a relative peace on the Korean peninsula for the later part of the twentieth century. The resources (means) committed to execute this strategy include a strong military presence for deterrence; near diplomatic isolation; enactment of economic trade sanctions and embargoes; and a sustained anti-North Korean informational campaign. Although not all-inclusive, the items listed above serve as the hallmarks of our current containment strategy.

New and emerging threats characterized by failed, rogue, or non-state actors (terrorists) possessing WMD and other technologies have created an ends, ways, and means mismatch. No longer can the U.S. predict with any level of certainty the time, place, and type of the next attack against our vital interests or those of our allies. This said, we must reexamine our current strategy towards North Korea and determine its applicability. Risks associated with not reassessing ends, ways, and means could result in catastrophic loss of life, global/regional economic devastation, regional instability, and loss of U.S. prestige and credibility.

Scholars, politicians, and military strategists have posited several alternatives to the current strategy of containment. These include: maintenance of the status quo except with absolute diplomatic and economic isolation (to include any humanitarian assistance); undermining the regime of Kim Jong Il through subversive means; a strategy of engagement – open and active dialogue with the North; and a strategy of "buying" our objectives – a policy seen by the Bush administration as nuclear blackmail by the North

Koreans.[2] As noted above, policymakers have been unable to achieve consensus on the best strategy to achieve our desired end states. In the absence of consensus, the long-standing strategy of containment has prevailed.

Clearly, the North represents a threat to U.S. vital interests on the Korean peninsula. This remains a perplexing dilemma. Though the strategy of containment has successfully prevented conflict for more than half a century, a new and dynamic environment threatens continued peace and regional security. This strategic research project will propose, compare and contrast, and recommend a U.S. strategy for effectively dealing with North Korea. The three strategies (courses of action) that will be examined include: (1) maintaining the status quo, (2) strategic withdrawal of U.S. forces form South Korea, and (3) a three-pronged strategy of containment, engagement, and regional alliances. The criteria used to compare and contrast each strategy are diplomatic acceptability, economic viability, and military feasibility. Each course of action and criteria used to evaluate the strategies will be discussed in further detail.

North Korea's strict adherence to established international laws and order is essenti al to the development of a secure and stable Asian-Pacific region. The strategy of containment, as originally developed, was successful in containing the spread of communism and preventing the conquest of South Korea by the North. However, recent efforts by North Korea to use nuclear weapons and proliferation as bargaining tools in order to secure its demands have severely undermined the strategy of containment as well as regional and worldwide security. Such actions require U.S. officials to review current strategies and change or amend them as necessary.

COURSES OF ACTION

Maintaining the status quo perpetuates the established strategy of containment. Political and economic isolation coupled with a strong U.S. military forward presence remains the cornerstone of this policy[3]. A limited "carrot and stick" approach such as providing North Korea with humanitarian aid and fuel oil shipments in exchange for its observance of international agreements, laws, and norms should be the extent of contact and negations between the U.S. and the North. Continuing to leverage the power of organizations such as the United Nations, World Trade Organization, International Monetary Fund, etc., against North Korea further legitimizes this U.S. strategy.

A second potential course of action is the strategic withdrawal of U.S. forces from South Korea. This strategy involves significantly enhancing South Korean military capabilities through foreign aid, military sales, training, and robust security assistance programs. The U.S. military

2

currently has 37,000 personnel assigned in Korea.[4] Under this newly proposed strategy, the majority of U.S. forces would be removed. Only vital logistical sites such as ports, facilities, and pre-positioned equipment and supplies would be maintained. Additionally, critical staff and liaison functions necessary to facilitate the rapid build-up of combat power, should a U.S. presence be required in the region, would be manned.

The final course of action proposed is a three-pronged strategy. It represents an adaptation of the current containment policy coupled with elements of engagement and support of regional actors. This strategy seeks to leverage the positive aspects of the current containment policy, while at the same time encouraging open and frank diplomatic and economic negotiations between North Korea, the U.S., and its allies (specifically South Korea, Japan, China, and Russia.)[5]

CRITERIA

How does one select an appropriate course of action for national leadership to follow? One method is to develop criterion to evaluate options. The criteria established to compare and contrast the proposed courses of action presented above include diplomatic acceptability, economic viability, and military feasibility. Diplomatic acceptability is expressed in terms of favorable support both domestically and abroad for our actions. Support of our allies, alliances, treaties, and international organizations are paramount to our success. They provide a basic framework from which to operate and help determine measures of acceptable behavior. Economic viability refers to responsible and sound monetary, fiscal, and trade policy. Finally, military feasibility relates to the ability of the U.S. to assure our allies, dissuade, deter, and decisively defeat any adversary.[6]

ANALYSIS OF COURSES OF ACTION

Using the established criteria as an evaluative tool, each course of action will be thoroughly analyzed and then compared and contrasted to one another in order to determine the most preferred solution. The final result of this analysis will be a recommendation to the national leadership on which course of action would best resolve the current Korean security dilemma. A detailed analysis of each of the three courses of action follows.

CONTAINMENT VS. STRATEGIC WITHDRAWAL

Diplomatically speaking, the U.S. containment policy towards North Korea has been successful since 1953. Furthermore, our strong presence has enabled us to exert our power as a global hegemon while attempting to set the conditions for success and favorably shape the region in terms of vital U.S. interests[7]. Strong political influence has also enabled us to isolate North Korea while simultaneously dealing with the emergence of China as a regional hegemon. As stated earlier, the new global environment demands that we reevaluate our current policy of containment. Despite containment's past effectiveness, North Korea has opted to revitalize its WMD production capability and proliferation efforts. No longer does the strategy of containment, specifically diplomatic isolation of the North, seem a viable option in itself. The criticism surrounding the Bush administration's containment strategy revolves around its well-established "non-negotiation" philosophy. This policy requires North Korea to immediately freeze and allow, through independent verification, proof of suspension of nuclear weapons development, presence of any WMD programs, and ballistic missile research, development, testing and exportation initiatives.[8] Until these specific demands have been met, the possibility of future dialogue towards peace and the reduction of tensions on the Korean peninsula seem unattainable.

In contrast to the containment strategy, strategic withdrawal of U.S. forces from South Korea poses a number of diplomatic dilemmas. Removal of forces could be viewed as the first step in deescalating tensions. North Korea views U.S. military presence as an act of potential aggression. Therefore, the North continuously demands a "bilateral nonaggression treaty" signed by the U.S. as a prerequisite for future peace.[9] Strategic withdrawal might be the catalyst for peace; however, it might also signal a weakening U.S. resolve and encourage further aggression by the North. On the other hand, removal of U.S. forces could evoke harsh diplomatic backlash from many of our allies and other Asian-Pacific regional actors. Current plans to reduce American troop deployments by 12,000 in Korea have met with significant resistance from Korean and Japanese officials.[10] South Korean diplomats have voiced concerns regarding North Korean aggression, regional stability, U.S. resolve, commitment to allies and alliances, and U.S. treaty obligations.[11] Furthermore, U.S. credibility and prestige would likely suffer resulting in a diminished capability to influence regional actors (primarily North Korea and China) and shape the region in terms of vital U.S. national interests.

The economic viability of the current U.S. containment policy towards North Korea remains basically sound. Stringent monetary and trade policies have devastated the North in an attempt to bring them into compliance with international norms, values, and laws. Through our status as a global superpower, the U.S. has been able to influence most of our allies, regional actors, and international organizations to support economic sanctions and embargoes against the North. These efforts have been largely successful until late. Leading experts posit that the underlying reason for the resurgence of the North's WMD program and proliferation efforts stems from the country's near economic devastation.[12] Sanctions and embargoes, coupled with a failing agrarian system have lead to mass starvation, malnourishment, and a potential humanitarian crisis. In order to offset current U.S. economic policies, North Korea has chosen to sell WMD technology and components in return for hard currency or drastically needed food and supplies. Other experts contend that while economic policies have achieved their desired impact, a humanitarian crisis could be avoided if the North Korean government redirects money from its massive army to the people. Currently, 33.9 percent of the countries gross domestic product (GDP) is allocated to military expenditures.[13] This said, current U.S. economic policy appears to have fostered an environment conducive to creating instability between the North Korean leadership, its army, and the people.

Strategic withdrawal of U.S. forces from South Korea would present some unique economic challenges for the United States. As discussed earlier, removal of forces might promote a peaceful solution that affords the U.S. and other regional actor's access to a new and emerging North Korean market. Although remotely possible, this is highly unlikely given the North's past history and aggressive nature. More than likely, the U.S. would lose global and regional credibility, unfettered access to the Asian-Pacific market, and the ability to influence regional economic policies. Our departure might also lead to reduced levels of foreign investment (other than by U.S.) due to security concerns. Loss of this foothold in the Asian-Pacific market would be cataclysmic to the U.S. economy. Approximately 25 percent of our annual imports come from this region.[14] In addition, the emergence of China as a potential global super power will require that the U.S. remain fully entrenched in this region in order to contain and shape China's ascendancy into the global marketplace.

In terms of military feasibility, the strategy of containment is executable. Our National Security Strategy of 1-4-2-1 (1 - homeland defense as first priority, 4 - maintaining deterrent forces forwardly deployed in four regions, 2 - the ability to swiftly defeat enemy efforts in two theaters of operations simultaneously, 1 - decisively defeating an adversary in one of the two theaters) supports the forward deployment of 37,000 personnel assigned to dissuade, deter, or defeat North Korean forces if called upon.[15] These forces represent the deterrent element of our containment strategy that has successfully maintained peace for over 50 years. Increased operational tempo, the Global War on Terror, transformation, and dwindling resources have

5

placed untold burden on our military forces. Regardless, the U.S. remains capable of deploying military forces anywhere and defending the vital interests of the U.S. and its allies. North Korea is no exception and the forward deployment of forces stationed on the peninsula signals our continuing commitment to our allies and also affords us the ability to rapidly respond to other contingencies within the region.

A strategic withdrawal of U.S. military forces from Korea would pose a considerable threat to South Korea without first enhancing the capability of its military or encouraging other regional actors to participate in its shared defense. As discussed earlier, significant investment in terms of foreign aid, military sales, training, and security assistance would be required. South Korea currently spends only 2.8 percent of its GDP on military expenditures.[16] Additionally, current U.S. power projection capability would not support the rapid build-up of combat power necessary to defeat an unambiguous, direct North Korean attack. As strategic lift and transformation initiatives evolve, U.S. forces will inevitably become more strategically deployable and less dependent on forward basing. This objective will not be realized for years to come; therefore, U.S. forces must either remain forward deployed or the ROK must be willing to drastically increase defense spending and assume higher levels of risk. Although possible to execute, strategic withdrawal would require considerable resources and lead-time, time that could be utilized for further development and proliferation of WMD by the North.

Table 1 depicts a comparison between the strategy of containment (COA 1) and the strategy of strategic withdrawal (COA 2). COA 1 is superior to COA 2. In a nutshell, the current strategy of containment has kept North Korea "in check" for over fifty years. This policy has been relatively successful in promoting regional stability, building alliances, and fostering economic prosperity. The principal advantage of COA 1 is its proven track record of success. However, new and expanding North Korean nuclear threats and proliferation efforts pose a serious challenge to this strategy. Likewise, a strategy of strategic withdrawal might or might not reduce tensions while at the same time signal to our friends and allies potential weakness, loss of resolve, and the demise of U.S. credibility and prestige worldwide. Therefore, containment is preferred over the strategy of withdrawal.

CRITERIA	COA 1	COA 2
DIPLOMATIC	+ Relative regional stability + Allies and international support + Isolates communist ideals - Lack of communications - No resolution of conflict - Isolation from democratic ideals	+ De-escalation of tensions * + Opens potential negotiations * - Loss of U.S. creditability - Loss of U.S. regional influence - U.S. perceived weak - Changing vital interests
CRITERIA	COA 1	COA 2
ECONOMIC	+ Isolates North's economy + Pressure forces North to negotiate + Effective sanctions/embargoes + Leverages international economies - Potential humanitarian crisis - WMD proliferation for money	+ Greater access to Asian-Pacific markets * + Enhances regional stability * + U.S. access to North's markets * - U.S. loss of foothold in region ** - Regional instability ** - Loss of U.S. credibility ** - Loss of U.S. revenue ** - Loss of influence on China **
MILITARY	+ Successfully prevented war + U.S. forward deterrent + Provides assurance to allies - Dedicated U.S. force - Lack of U.S. military strategic flexibility	+ U.S. military strategic flexibility + Enhanced ROK self-defense forces + ROK defense shared by regional actors - Potential resumption of hostilities - Loss of U.S. military influence in region - Loss of U.S. military influence on China

TABLE 1. COA 1 & 2 COMPARISON MATRIX

* If strategic withdrawal results in successful conflict resolution

** If strategic withdrawal results in North Korean aggression

CONTAINMENT VS. THREE-PRONGED STRATEGY

The United States, through its diplomatic arm, has effectively garnered the support of the international community and isolated North Korea. While containing the North, the U.S. has continued to foster diplomatic relations with key regional actors such as South Korea, Japan, Russia, and China. These actions further solidify the legitimacy of U.S. efforts and promote regional stability. However, recent developments indicate that North Korea intends to "up the ante" by resuming its WMD development program and proliferation efforts. These activities are seen by the North as the best way to "exact aid and concessions from the rest of the world"[17] – the equivalent of blackmail. This new dynamic exposes one of the most significant weaknesses of the containment strategy – time. The more time it takes for North Korea to comply with U.S. and international law, the more time available for it to develop and proliferate WMD. Diplomatic isolation of North Korea prevents reconciliatory dialogue between the two sides. A stalemate or delay favors the underlying efforts of the North.

Adoption of the three-pronged strategy would help resolve many of the issues mentioned above. This strategy represents an adaptation of the current containment policy coupled with elements of selective engagement and support of regional actors. An obvious advantage of this strategy would be engagement of the North by U.S. diplomats. In order to be successful, the U.S. administration must be willing to openly engage North Korean officials. Without a conduit for open and frank dialogue, each side will continue to harbor their respective feelings of mistrust and grievances. Scholars and foreign affairs experts suggest that the primary stumbling block between the two countries is extremely limited and ineffective communications. Although severely hampered by the Bush administration's policy of diplomatic isolation, both sides talk but neither listens. Succinctly stated, North Korea's mistrust of the U.S. and her allies combined with the Bush administration's immediate dismissal of all North Korean points of views and issues prevents any and all hopes of a compromise.[18] This "talking past" one another must be resolved if a viable solution is to be obtained. Embracing a policy of engagement is the solution. Formally establishing and publicly portraying a willingness to engage diplomatically with North Korean government officials could serve as a catalyst for peace. Not only should the U.S. develop a direct diplomatic link with the North, they should also convince other key regional actors to participate in the development of a "regional solution" to the ongoing security issue. These negotiations and discussions should be frank, open, and scheduled on a continuous basis in an attempt to reduce mistrust between parties; promote mutual understanding of both sides' issues and reservations; attain a proposed solution to ease and eliminate tension; and develop a mutually agreed upon plan of action to implement such solutions. Although some might regard such a policy of engagement as being overly optimistic, a continued narrow-minded strategy of containment leading to simply more of the status quo favors the North. Again, time is the ally of evil and the enemy of good. A policy of engagement does not signify weakness or a willingness on behalf of the Bush administration to "buy U.S. interests."[19] Rather, it must be formulated and executed with the goal of opening honest dialogue from that compromise follows.

Assistance of all regional actors in the peaceful resolution of issues on the Korean peninsula benefits all involved. Although the Korean crisis represents a unique Asian-Pacific regional issue with vital U.S. national interests at stake, the U.S. should not attempt to pursue or negotiate a resolution unilaterally. As stated in the latest version of the National Security Strategy (2002): "[w]e are guided by the conviction that no nation can build a safer, better world alone. Alliance and multilateral institutions can multiply the strength of freedom-loving nations. The United States is committed to lasting institutions like the United Nations, the World Trade Organization, the Organization of American States, and NATO as well as other long-standing alliances."[20] Leveraging the power gained by involving all the regional actors is the optimal solution. This in turn enhances open and frank dialogue; sensitivity and better understanding of cultural diversity; alliances and bonds between nation states; development of mutually agreed upon courses of actions; execution, oversight, and enforcement of agreed solutions; sharing of resources; and legitimacy. As positive as this may sound, the most difficult aspect of this strategy to achieve will be obtaining consensus. The time necessary to conduct these negotiations could also be lengthy.

The U.S. containment policy towards North Korea remains economically viable, but at a cost. Although a successful strategy in the past, indicators reveal that our current policies are propelling North Korea to the brink of a humanitarian crisis. Economic devastation, famine, and malnutrition may further threaten the relatively fragile balance of power on the peninsula.[21] As noted earlier, some experts blame the current U.S. administration and its strategy of containment for the resurgence of the North's WMD program. Continued implementation of both economic and trade sanctions remain easily executable; however, a resulting humanitarian crisis would devastate the region, undermine our current strategy, and erode our credibility both regionally and worldwide.

Utilizing the three-pronged strategy of containment, engagement, and regional actors would offer many economic advantages over our current policy. First, through a process of engagement the administration could adopt a more flexible posture utilizing a "carrot and stick" approach as a means of resolving issues.[22] Providing incentives for desired North Korean

9

behaviors, such as humanitarian aid or fuel oil shipments in exchange for WMD development and proliferation cessation, might resurrect successful negotiation talks. Second, regional actors stringent support of U.S. economic and trade policies towards North Korea would help force the North's compliance to acceptable international norms and values. Third, a regional solution to the security issue promotes economic burden sharing while simultaneously allowing continued U.S. access to Asian-Pacific markets. Fourth, involvement of the U.S. and regional actors in a mutually agreed upon strategy strengthens the credibility, prestige, and ability of the U.S. to shape the region in terms favorable to its vital national interests.[23] Again, the primary drawback of this strategy is the inability to obtain consensus and the time required to develop and implement the agreed upon solution.

Forward deployed U.S. military forces on the Korean peninsula, backed up by additional forces in Japan, have long been the bastions of our current containment policy. Their presence signifies resolve, commitment to our allies, and deterrence. Although not the only element of power used to coerce North Korea, this remains the most persuasive and visible tool used to moderate potential aggression. Forward presence enables the U.S. to rapidly respond to crises while promoting regional stability. The primary disadvantage of this strategy is the requirement to maintain a dedicated military presence in the region. These forces are thus unavailable to respond to other worldwide contingencies.

Adoption of the three-pronged strategy could alleviate some of the burden placed on current U.S. military forces. Regional actors involvement in the formulation of a military alliance designed to deter and defeat North Korean aggression would be the optimal solution. Regional actors could also equally share the requirements for resources in terms of manpower, dollars, equipment, and training. Other advantages of this strategy include: a multilateral versus a unilateral approach to conflict resolution; a potential de-escalation of tensions resulting from reduced U.S. military presence; greater U.S. military strategic flexibility; and increased pressure exerted by unified regional actors designed to compel North Korea to comply with international law and order. This regional alliance would help secure vital interests of the U.S. and its allies, a critical component of our current National Security Strategy. [24] Furthermore, operations devoid of multilateral or regional alliance support have predominately failed or become too resource-intensive to execute. For example, critics contend that the Bush administration's decision to conduct offensive operations against Iraq was done unilaterally, in their eyes. Failure to obtain United Nations' backing prior to the commencement of hostilities left the credibility and image of the U.S. somewhat tarnished. Although viewed as a great militarily success, the resulting quagmire brought on by requirements, such as peace keeping and nation building operations,

10

might well have been avoided through enhanced support from other countries. Lessons learned from Operation Iraqi Freedom, as well as in Bosnia and Kosovo, suggest that future U.S./North Korea policies should optimize the benefits of strong regional actor and alliance support. The difficulty with this course of action lies, once again, in the ability of the United States to garner the required support, gain consensus, and equably distribute the burden amongst actors. All this must be achieved while remaining responsive to our treaty obligations and continuing to secure our own vital interests worldwide.

Table 2 depicts a comparison between the strategy of containment (COA 1) and the three-pronged strategy (COA 3). Using the previously identified criteria, the comparison clearly indicates COA 3 is a better option. It promotes a regional solution to the Korean security dilemma. This option enables the U.S. to assert its role as a world hegemon while subsequently continuing to shape the region in terms favorable to the U.S. Not only does this course of action afford the greatest opportunity for regional stability, it also enables the United States to shape the emergence of China as an upcoming regional and potential world super power.

CRITERIA	COA 1	COA 3
DIPLOMATIC	+ Relative regional stability + Allies and international support + Isolation of communist ideals - Lack of communications - No resolution of conflict - Isolation from democratic ideals	+ Open lines of communications + Regional support + International support + Regional stability + Exposure to democratic ideals + U.S. maintains regional influence - Perceived as buying U.S. interests - Difficulty in gaining regional consensus
ECONOMIC	+ Isolates North's economy + Pressure forces North to negotiate + Effective sanctions and embargoes + Leverages international economies - Potential humanitarian crisis - WMD proliferation for money	+ Greater regional stability + Alleviation of humanitarian crisis + Greater access to Korean markets + Exposure to capitalistic ideals + Greater pressure on North to comply with international norms + Greater burden sharing by allies + U.S. maintains regional influence

11

CRITERIA	COA 1	COA 3
		- Obtaining consensus
		- Time intensive
		- Loss of U.S. sovereignty
MILITARY	+ Successfully prevented war + U.S. forward deterrent + Provides assurance to allies - Dedicated U.S. force - Lack of U.S. military strategic flexibility	+ Regional actors share ROK defense + Formulation of regional military alliances + Multilateral versus unilateral + Enhanced ROK self defense + De-escalation of tensions with North + Greater U.S. military strategic flexibility + Regional pressure for North to comply with international will - Gaining consensus - Time intensive - Loss of U.S. military force presence

TABLE 2. COA 1 & 3 COMPARISON MATRIX

STRATEGIC WITHDRAWAL VS. THREE-PRONGED STRATEGY

While removal of U.S. forces from Korea might reduce tensions with the North, such an action could adversely affect current diplomatic relations between the U.S. and its Asian-Pacific allies. Departure of forces could signify a change in U.S. commitment and throw the region into total disarray. Lack of U.S. presence as a stabilizing force might encourage South Korea to align itself with China as a means of protection and support. This potential alignment would degrade our ability to diplomatically influence the region and contain China as it begins to emerge as a future regional/global super power and chief competitor.

Conversely, the three-pronged strategy promotes an atmosphere conducive to open dialogue, negotiation, and mutual conflict resolution between all members of the regional alliance. Furthermore, this strategy unifies the efforts of all parties involved and helps in the development of a "regional solution" to the problem as opposed to a U.S. dictated solution, the end result being a more palatable option for the North. Recent six-party diplomatic talks that took place in October 2003, between North Korea and the Asian-Pacific alliance strongly support the validity of this organization and a desire to obtain a regional solution to this dilemma.[25] As noted before, the difficulty with this course of action revolves around the issue of gaining consensus and initiating action in a timely manner. Regional or a multilateral approach to conflict resolution is clearly superior to the unilateral strategy of containment.

The economic advantages associated with the strategic withdrawal of forces from the Korean peninsula would consist of reduced costs associated with maintaining a forward presence and potential access to North Korean markets should a U.S. withdrawal facilitate future peace. Likewise, the disadvantages far outweigh the advantages should our withdrawal result in a resumption of conflict. Removal of forces would also signal a change in U.S. resolve, no doubt influencing both regional and economic stability. The historical conquest of South Korea by Japan makes it possible that Korea would align itself with China for economic and security support if needed. Loss of U.S. credibility, prestige, and influence in the Asian-Pacific region could rapidly follow.

The three-pronged strategy affords the U.S. a myriad of economic options from which to deal with North Korea. First, the policy of engagement enables both sides a venue to air respective grievances and demands. Adoption of an economic "carrot and stick" methodology that both rewards and punishes the North for selected behavior has been suggested as the best approach to jumpstart stalled negotiations between all parties. Second, formulation of a regional alliance further leverages the power of all actors to influence the desired behavior of the North. Third, as stated earlier, a regional solution to the current issue would help promote regional and economic stability, establish legitimacy, and more equally share the economic burden currently shouldered by both the U.S. and South Korea. Finally, establishment of such an alliance would enable the United States to exercise its role as world hegemon while continuing to maintain unimpeded access to global markets and economies.

Strategic withdrawal from the Korean peninsula without significant enhancement to existing ROK forces represents an unacceptable risk. Although removal of forces would offer increased U.S. military strategic flexibility, the potential losses far outnumber the gains. In order to execute this strategy, significant resources would be needed in terms of dollars, equipment, and training to properly offset current ROK shortfalls. The time required to affect this change would also be significant.

The synergies gained through the formulation of a regional Asian-Pacific military alliance underscore the relative advantages of the three-pronged strategy. Support by regional actors would allow greater unity of military effort; mutually agreed upon military goals and objectives; unified pressure exerted on North Korea to conform; greater debt and military burden-sharing amongst members; and enhanced U.S. military strategic flexibility. The creation of this alliance

13

would not only serve as a unifying force but would also secure the "buy-in" of all parties in order to develop, implement, and execute a regionally developed strategy to resolve the Korean security dilemma. An additional benefit is the greater potential for acceptance by the North of a regional solution versus a U.S. mandate. Greater burden-sharing by others members of the alliance would enable U.S. forces to shrink their current footprint of 37,000 personnel. More aggressively, the complete withdrawal of all personnel, minus those needed to maintain key logistical infrastructure and liaison, might be feasible in the future. Worst case, should the U.S. decide to maintain its forward presence, forces would now be able to deploy in support of other regional crises. Under the current strategy of containment this is not possible today. The greatest impediment to this course of action is the inability to gain support, consensus, and implement action in a timely manner. Though a daunting task, the potential benefits associated with this regional alliance makes this course of action an extremely viable strategy.

Table 3 depicts a comparison between the strategy of strategic withdrawal (COA 2) and the three-pronged strategy (COA 3). Using the previously identified criteria, the comparison once again indicates the overall superiority of COA 3. This strategy represents an adaptation of our current containment policy coupled with elements of engagement and the formulation of regional alliances. Once again, COA 3 offers a "regional" solution to the North Korean issue. It also enables the United States to remain actively engaged in the conflict resolution process while continuously shaping the Asian-Pacific region in terms favorable to our vital national interests.

CRITERIA	COA 2	COA 3
DIPLOMATIC	+ De-escalation of tensions + Opens potential negotiations - Loss of U.S. credibility - Loss of U.S. regional influence - U.S. perceived as weak - Changing vital interest	+ Open lines of communications + Regional support + International support + Regional stability + Exposure to democratic ideals + U.S. maintains regional influence - Perceived as buying U.S. interests - Difficulty in gaining regional consensus

CRITERIA	COA 2	COA 3
ECONOMIC	+ Greater access to Asian-Pacific markets * + Enhances regional stability * + U.S. access to North's markets * - U.S. loss of foothold in region ** - Regional instability ** - Loss of U.S. credibility ** - Loss of U.S. credibility ** - Loss of influence on China **	+ Greater regional stability + Alleviation of humanitarian crisis + Greater access to Korean markets + Exposure to capitalistic ideals + Greater pressure on North to comply with international norms + Greater burden sharing by allies + U.S. maintains regional influence - Obtaining consensus - Time intensive - Loss of U.S. sovereignty
MILITARY	+ U.S. military strategic flexibility + Enhanced ROK self-defense + ROK defense shared by regional actors - Potential resumption of hostilities - Loss of U.S. military influence in region - Loss of U.S. military influence on China	+ Regional shared ROK defense + Formulation of regional military alliances + Multilateral versus unilateral + Enhanced ROK self defense + De-escalation of tensions with North + Greater U.S. military strategic flexibility + Regional pressure for North to comply with international will - Gaining consensus - Time intensive - Loss of U.S. military force presence

TABLE 3. COA 2 & 3 COMPARISON MATRIX

* If strategic withdrawal results in successful conflict resolution

** If strategic withdrawal results in North Korean aggression

CONCLUSION

The Post-World War II strategy of containment can no longer be universally applied as the policy of choice on the Korean peninsula. Although still a valid concept, emergence of failed nation states and terrorist organizations armed with WMD or other harmful technologies drastically influences global security. The time and choosing of our enemy's next attack against the vital interests of the U.S. and its allies is no longer predictable. Those who threaten, support, or enable such activities must be dealt with both effectively and immediately. Such is the case with North Korea. The purpose of this paper was to conduct an analysis of current U.S. policy towards North Korea and recommend necessary changes as applicable. As mentioned earlier, the basic policy of containment still provides a sound foundation from which to further develop and refine necessary foreign policy and strategy. That said, it is my belief that the U.S. should adopt a new and more comprehensive three-pronged strategy to deal with the security issue presented on the Korean peninsula. Containment through deterrence, a policy of engagement, and co-opting regional actors and alliances to promote U.S. security efforts are the keys to peace on the Korean peninsula and protection of U.S. vital interests world-wide.

Recent developments such as the six party talks may finally signal a willingness on behalf of all parties to peacefully resolve the Korean security dilemma. Resumption of dialogue (engagement) coupled with the involvement of U.S., South Korea, North Korea, Japan, Russia, and China (regional actors) not only represents a change in basic U.S. strategy but also signifies a concerted effort on behalf of the current administration to resolve this long-standing security issue. Adoption of the proposed three-pronged strategy (containment, engagement, and regional actors/alliances) is the appropriate policy for peace.

WORD COUNT = 5966

ENDNOTES

[1]Lynn Davis, and Jeremy Shapiro, "The U.S. Army and the New National Security Strategy." (Rand Arroyo Center, 2003), 87.

[2]William J. Perry, "Review of United States Policy Toward North Korea: Findings and Recommendations." Available from <http://www.state.gov/www/regions/eap/991012 _northkorea_rpt.html>. Internet. Accessed 15 September 2003.

[3]John Pomfret, "North Korean Threats Played Down by U.S.; As Talks End, Sides Agree to Reconvene," The Washington Times, 31 August 2003, sec. A, p. 18.

[4]Robert Burns, "Fewer Gis Likely in S. Korea," The Associated Press, 18 September 2003; available from http://www.korea.army.mil; Internet; accessed 18 September 2003.

[5]Barbara Demick, "The World; N. Korea Says It Will Return to Arms Talks; China reports that Pyongyang has pledged to rejoin the six-party negotiations in an effort to reach a solution on its nuclear program," Los Angles Times, 31 October 2003, sec. A, p. 3.

[6]Donald H. Rumsfeld, Quadrennial Defense Review Report (Washington, D.C.: The Secretary of Defense, 30 September 2001), III-IV.

[7]Henry A. Kissinger, "America at the Apex: Empire or Leader," (New York, NY: Simon & Schuster, 2001), p 17-31.

[8]Nicholas Mele, "The North Korean Conundrum." America, 8 September 2003, 18.

[9]Anthony Faiola, "N. Korea Agrees To Resume Nuclear Talks; U.S. Reacts Coolly to Demand for Simultaneous Actions," The Washington Post, 31 October 2003, p. A.18.

[10]Burns, 1.

[11]Ibid.

[12]Mele,18.

[13]Central Intelligence Agency, "The World Factbook – North Korea." World Factbook Online August 2003; available from<http:www.cia.gov/cia/publications/factbook/geos/kn.html>; Internet; accessed 5 November 2003.

[14]Central Intelligence Agency, "The World Factbook – United States." World Factbook Online August 2003; available fr om <http:www.cia.gov/cia/publications/factbook/print/us.html>; Internet; accessed 5 November 2003.

[15]Rumsfeld, 17-23

[16]Central Intelligence Agency, "The World Factbook – South Korea." World Factbook Online August 2003; available from <http:www.cia.gov/cia/publications/factbook/print/ks.html>; Internet; accessed 5 November 2003.

[17]Central Intelligence Agency, "North Korea Can Skip Nuclear Talks," Associated Press, 9 November 2003; available from <http://www.foxnews.com/printer_story_/0,3566,102584,00.html>; Internet; accessed 9 November 2003.

[18]Mele, 23.

[19]Perry, 2.

[20]George Bush, The National Security Strategy of the United States of America. (Washington, D.C.: The White House, September 2002).

[21]Central Intelligence Agency, "The World Factbook – North Korea," 7.

[22]Stan Crock, and Rose Brady, "North Korea: Talking is One Thing. Getting Somewhere is Another," Business Week, 25 August 2003, Iss. 3846, p. 59.

[23]Kissinger, 17-31.

[24]Bush, 5-7.

[25]Faiola, A.18.

BIBLIOGRAPHY

Barone, Michael. "Stopping Rogue Nukes." U.S. News and World Report, vol 35, issue, 3, (2003): 27.

Bennett, Cortlan, and Melinda Liu. "Nukes and Crime: China's Borderline Troubles." Newsweek, 1 September 2003, 5.

Brodie, Bernard. "The Test of Korea." War and Politics. New York: Macmillan Publishing, 1973.

Burns, Robert. "Fewer GIs Likely in S. Korea," Associated Press, 18 September 2003; available from http://www.korea.army.mil; Internet; accessed 18 September 2003.

Bush, George W. National Strategy for Homeland Security. Washington, D.C.: The White House, July 2002.

Bush, George. National Strategy for Combating Terrorism. Washington, D.C.: The White House, February 2003.

Bush, George. The National Security Strategy of the United States of America. Washington, D.C.: The White House, September 2002.

Central Intelligence Agency. "North Korea Can Skip Nuclear Talks." Associated Press, 9 November 2003. Available from <http://www.foxnews.com/printer_story_/0,3566,102584,00. html>. Internet. Accessed 9 November 2003.

Central Intelligence Agency. "The World Factbook – China." World Factbook Online August 2003. Available from<http:www.cia.gov/cia/publications/factbook/print/ch.html>. Internet. Accessed 5 November 2003.

Central Intelligence Agency. "The World Factbook – Japan." World Factbook Online August 2003. Available from<http:www.cia.gov/cia/publications/factbook/print/ja.html>. Internet. Accessed 5 November 2003.

Central Intelligence Agency. "The World Factbook – North Korea." World Factbook Online August 2003. Available from<http:www.cia.gov/cia/publications/factbook/geos/kn.html>. Internet. Accessed 5 November 2003.

Central Intelligence Agency. "The World Factbook – Russia." World Factbook Online August 2003. Available from<http:www.cia.gov/cia/publications/factbook/print/rs.html>. Internet. Accessed 5 November 2003.

Central Intelligence Agency. "The World Factbook – South Korea." World Factbook Online August 2003. Available from <http:www.cia.gov/cia/publications/factbook/print/ks.html>. Internet. Accessed 5 November 2003.

Central Intelligence Agency. "The World Factbook – United States." World Factbook Online August 2003. Available from <http:www.cia.gov/cia/publications/factbook/print/us.html>. Internet. Accessed 5 November 2003.

Crock, Stan, and Rose Brady. "North Korea: Talking is One Thing. Getting Somewhere is Another." Business Week, 25 August 2003, Iss. 3846, pg 59.

Davis, Lynn, and Jeremy Shapiro. "The U.S. Army and the New National Security Strategy." Rand Arroyo Center, 2003, 85-107.

Demick, Barbra. "The World; N. Korea Says It Will Return to Arms Talks; China reports that Pyongyang has pledged to rejoin the six-party negotiations in an effort to reach a solution on its nuclear program," Los Angles Times, 31 October 2003, sec. A, p. 3.

Faiola, Anthony. "N. Korea Agrees To Resume Nuclear Talks; U.S. Reacts Coolly to Demand for Simultaneous Actions." The Washington Post, 31 October 2003, sec. A, p. 18.

Faiola, Anthony. "What Do They Want in South Korea? Unification!" The Washington Post, 8 September 2003, sec. A, p. 1.

Fairclough, Gordon. "Defector Advocates Regime Change for North Korea." The Wall Street Journal, 28 October 2003, sec. A, p.14.

Fairclough, Gordon. "The Family Saga of Kim Jong II Sheds Light on Dictatorship." The Wall Street Journal, 10 October 2003, sec A16, p.1.

Jablonsky, David. "Strategic Vision and Presidential Authority in the Post-Cold War Era." Parameters (Winter 1991-1992): 2-15.

Jisi, Wang. "A View from China." Foreign Policy (Jul/Aug 2003): 31-32.

Kahn, Joseph. "Chinese Aide Says U.S. is Obstacle in Korean Talks." New York Times, September 2003, sec. A, p.3.

Kemp, Fredrick, and David Cloud. "Baghdad Records Show Hussein Sought Missiles, Other Aid Abroad." The Wall Street Journal, 3 November 2003, sec. A, p. 1.

Kirkpatrick, Melanie. "Unwelcome Truths." The Wall Street Journal, 28 October 2003, sec. A, p. 16.

Mele, Nicholas. "The North Korean Conundrum." America, 8 September 2003, 18-23.

Perry, William J. "Review of United States Policy Toward North Korea: Findings and Recommendations." Available from <http://www.state.gov/www/regions/eap/991012 _northkorea_rpt.html>. Internet. Accessed 15 September 2003.

Pomfret, John. "North Korean Threats Played Down by U.S.; As Talks End, Sides Agree To Reconvene." Washington Post, 31 August 2003, sec A, p. 18.

Sanger, David. "Rice Faults Past Administrations on Terror." The New York Times, 31 October 2003, sec. A. p. 6.

Sanger, David. "U.S. Said to Shift Approach in Talks with North Korea." New York Times, 5 September 2003, sec A, p.1.

Shin, Kim D. "The ROK - U.S. Alliance: Where is it Headed?" Strategic Forum 197 (April 2003): 1-4.

Slavin, Barbra, and Tom Squitieri. " On N. Korea, Answers are Elusive; A Diplomatic Diplomatic Breakthrough is Unlikely, a War would be Destructive, and Status Quo is Unacceptable." USA Today, 27 August 2003, p. A06.

Rumsfeld, Donald. Quadrennial Defense Review Report. Washington,D.C.: Defense Department, September 2003.

"United States: All the President's Fault?; Lexington." The Economist, 4 January 2003: p. 38.

U.S. – China Security Review Commission. Report to Congress: The National Security Implications of the Economic Relationship between the U.S. and China (Washington, D.C.: U.S. Government Printing Office, 2002), 15-33.

Weisman, Steven. "Bush Foreign Policy." New York Times, 5 September 2003, sec A, p.1.